CONTENTS

LIGHTHOUSES

The sea can be extremely dangerous, especially for people sailing at night. Many boats have been wrecked on rocks hidden below the water.

A long time ago people lit bonfires on the shore to warn sailors about dangerous stretches of coastline. But these warning beacons could not be seen from far away.

What was needed was a much brighter fire, or light, on a tall tower so that it could be seen for miles. This was called a lighthouse.

Sometimes people deliberately confused sailors. Look at the plan to see how wreckers tried to trick ships into following the wrong lights.

To avoid mistakes, a flashing lighthouse was invented by William Hutchinson in 1752. It turned round so that a narrow beam of light swung round, flashing past regularly.

Now every lighthouse gives out a different number of flashes at different speeds.

Why do you think it is important for every lighthouse to be different?

In 1756, John Smeaton designed the Eddystone Lighthouse which stands on a rock in the English Channel. (It was rebuilt in 1882).

When the weather is too bad for sailors to see them, lighthouses also sound a **foghorn**.

Modern lighthouses are operated by computers. They used to be worked by lighthouse-keepers.

The lamp room of a modern lighthouse.

COLOURS AND FEELINGS

Colour expressions

She was

'browned' off   'red' with anger   'green' with envy   'thinking green'

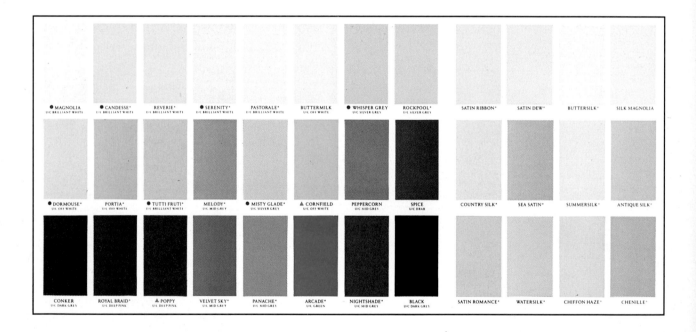

● MAGNOLIA U/C BRILLIANT WHITE	● CANDESSE* U/C BRILLIANT WHITE	REVERIE* U/C BRILLIANT WHITE

● MAGNOLIA U/C BRILLIANT WHITE   ● CANDESSE* U/C BRILLIANT WHITE   REVERIE* U/C BRILLIANT WHITE   ● SERENITY* U/C BRILLIANT WHITE   PASTORALE* U/C BRILLIANT WHITE   BUTTERMILK U/C OFF WHITE   ● WHISPER GREY U/C SILVER GREY   ROCKPOOL* U/C SILVER GREY   SATIN RIBBON*   SATIN DEW*   BUTTERSILK*   SILK MAGNOLIA

● DORMOUSE* U/C OFF WHITE   PORTIA* U/C OFF WHITE   ● TUTTI FRUTI* U/C BRILLIANT WHITE   MELODY* U/C MID GREY   ● MISTY GLADE* U/C SILVER GREY   ▲ CORNFIELD U/C OFF WHITE   PEPPERCORN U/C MID GREY   SPICE U/C DRAB   COUNTRY SILK*   SEA SATIN*   SUMMERSILK*   ANTIQUE SILK*

CONKER U/C DARK GREY   ROYAL BRAID* U/C DEEP PINK   ▲ POPPY U/C DEEP PINK   VELVET SKY* U/C MID GREY   PANACHE* U/C MID GREY   ARCADE* U/C GREEN   NIGHTSHADE* U/C MID GREY   BLACK U/C DARK GREY   SATIN ROMANCE*   WATERSILK*   CHIFFON HAZE*   CHENILLE*

Have you ever had a problem when you tried to describe a colour to someone?

Paint manufacturers try to think of really attractive names for paints to persuade people to buy them. It's not very easy to think of new and interesting names for colours.

> **Try it out for yourself. Find three colours around you and try to invent your own names for them.**

Colours

Red is a rose radiant with love,
Or red can be anger waiting to explode.
It is a robin searching for food,
Or is it the heart pumping furiously.

Orange is the furiousness of fire,
It is a juicy fruit waiting to be picked.
It is a blazing sunset sitting on a hill,
The tenderness of a new-born baby as well.

Brown is the colour of a meek foal,
Brown is the feeling of hope inside its mother.
It is the prickliness of hay it stumbles on,
And it's the warmth and comfort of his mother's body.

Blue is the calmness of the waves on the sea,
Of the sky with cotton-wool balls.
It's the thrashing of a shark eating its meal,
And the warbling song of the bluetit.

Green is the swaying of grass in the wind,
The glory of a peacock's tail shooting up.
The leaves blown off a tree.
And a feeling deep down inside.

Yellow sways gently when it's wheat,
It raves viciously when lava beneath the earth.
It covers the crabs under the sand.
It is the sun which cloaks the earth in its beams.

by Thomas Boldrin, age 10.
St Theresa's, East End Road, Finchley.

Pamela sees brown ... or red ... or orange

I was woken up at 3 o'clock in the morning by the sound of breaking glass and a burglar alarm ringing loudly. I jumped out of bed and rushed to the window to see what was happening. The glass part of the shop door opposite had been smashed and a man was coming out, carrying a huge pile of clothes. A few seconds later – out came a second and then a third. They piled the stolen clothes into a car parked under the orange street light and jumped in. I made a note of some details. The car, the colour, the number plate so I could tell the police. The next day I called the police – 'These men got into a car – it may have been red, orange, gold or brown and I couldn't read the number plate.'

What confusion did the orange street lights cause Pamela?

Next time you are out at night, have a look at the colours in the street.

You could make your own coloured scene using a box like this.

Use a shoebox without a lid

Cut out a small window at one end

Put your object in the box

Cover with coloured tissue paper

In the theatre, they use this idea to create special effects.

Which colours would you use to create:
● a spooky scene
● a warm feeling
● morning.

DOTTY PICTURES

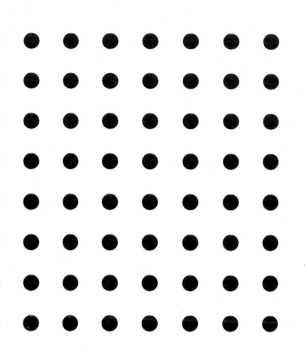

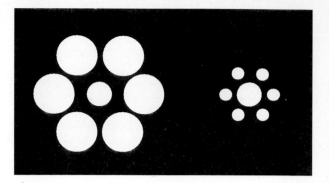

▲
Look at the white circles in the centre of each pattern.
Are they the same size?
Measure them to check your answer.

◀ What pattern do you see when you look at these dots? Look at them for a while until you see a pattern.
Do your friends see the same pattern?

A famous French artist called ▶ Georges Seurat painted many pictures like this one, using thousands of tiny dots.

He built up his pictures from painting thousands of tiny dots on his canvases. This kind of painting is called **pointillism** – point is the French word for dot. If you look at the picture from a distance you will see it differently from looking at it closely using a hand lens.

Pictures in newspapers, books, and magazines are also made up of dots. You might like to look at some of these pictures using a hand lens.

Did you know that the colour pictures on a TV screen are made from red, blue, or green dots?

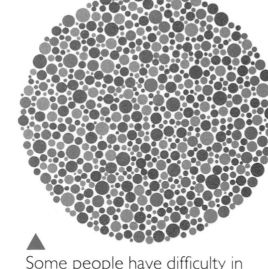

Some people have difficulty in seeing certain colours. What number do you see on this dot picture? The answer is at the bottom of the page.

Answer: If you are not colour-blind you will see a 5. If you can see a different number you may have difficulty in seeing some colours.

9

I know! In the bike lamp there's a kind of mirror behind the bulb - we could try using that to flash a signal with while the sun's out. How does SOS go in Morse Code? It's ...---... isn't it?

It is starting to get dark. We could use the bike lamps like they do in films. We could wave them backwards and forwards, or flash SOS with them like the mirror.

In the olden days they used to build bonfires to signal with at night. Maybe we should try to light a fire.

But we haven't any matches - and anyway, look at that sign. It says 'NO FIRES'.

NO FIRES

Prop up the bikes, then, if we fall asleep the rescue team's headlights or torches will pick out the reflectors and those bright luminous strips. We should wear our reflector bands too.

Children rescued from hillside
Hillwalkers see luminous reflectors

You might like to try out some of the ideas Susan and John thought of. You could turn the story into a play.

11

MAKING MOVING PICTURES

Some people call films 'movies' which is short for 'moving pictures'. Moving pictures are made from hundreds of separate pictures on a long see-through strip of film. The film runs through a projector which flashes each picture in turn onto a screen. Each picture shows a different part of the people's movements and the movements of the animals, cars, trees, waves or anything else.

Because the film moves so quickly your eyes don't see the separate pictures and as you watch it looks as if everything is moving.

In the days before cinema and television people made other kinds of moving pictures.

You could try to make your own moving pictures using one of these ideas as a starting point.

You could make your zoetrope out of a strip of cardboard like this, and spin it on an old pan lid.

draw something moving across your cardboard strip

A **zoetrope** was a toy that showed a moving picture. You can see one in this picture, taken at the Museum of the Moving Image in London. On the table are some cartoon strips. You put one of these round the inside of the zoetrope. Look through one of the slits as you spin the zoetrope and you should see the picture moving.

Flick books were also popular.

cardboard strip

pan lid

look through the slits as you spin your zoetrope

To make a flick book, draw a cartoon sequence on numbered squares of paper. The squares should be about 4 cm wide. Put them in order, then staple them together at the left-hand edge. You have made a little book. Now flick the pages and see your cartoon move.

CYCLING TO SCHOOL

14

PUTTING LIGHT ON PAPER

It is quite difficult to show light in pictures.

If you were drawing a picture, how would you show light from the sun or a torch?

If you were painting a picture, would you do it in the same way?

You could try out some ideas to see what happens.

Photographs can also show light in different ways.

Can you think of some words to describe the way light looks in the pictures on these pages?

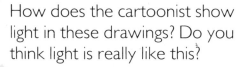

How does the cartoonist show light in these drawings? Do you think light is really like this?

LOOK AGAIN

Are you sure this picture is the right way up?
Which one is the real tree and which is the **reflection**?

How many dancers are putting on their ballet shoes?

How did the
photographer manage
to take this picture? ▶

◀ Where are the clouds in this
picture?

This picture shows a **shadow**
and a reflection. Which one is
the shadow? Which is the
reflection? What do you think
is the difference between them? ▶

Think of some more words or sayings to do with light and seeing.

USING LIGHT

Some supermarket entrances have a little gate which opens automatically when you approach it. How does it know you are coming? There is a beam of light shining on a light sensor. If you walk through it, you prevent the light beam from falling on the sensor. This makes the gate open. The light is placed low down so that even very small people cross the beam of light.

The same system is used for burglar alarms. When the beam of light is blocked, it might turn on a searchlight or make an alarm bell ring.

A television remote controller uses an invisible light beam (infra-red). The beam turns on and off very rapidly. This on-off sequence is different for each instruction. The detector in the television set can read these instructions and adjust the set accordingly.

Bar codes on different products can be 'read' using light. Light is reflected off the bar code onto a sensor which reads it as a series of ons and offs. The computer in the till interprets this as a sequence of numbers which is the code for that particular product. From the code, the computer can tell the price of the item and this is added to the bill.

How does a deaf person know that someone is ringing their doorbell? They can have a flashing light as well as a bell.

23

GLOSSARY

Flick book

A flick book is a booklet with a series of pictures which seem to move when you turn the pages rapidly.

Foghorn

A foghorn is a horn which makes a noise that travels a long way. Ships use them to warn others that they are approaching.

Pointillism

This is painting using small spots of colour. These spots blend together when you look at them from a distance so that you cannot see the individual spots.

Reflection

If you look into something shiny, like a mirror or a pool of water, you will see a picture of yourself. This is a reflection.

Shadow

If you shine a light on a wall and then put something, like your hand, between the light and the wall, you will see a shadow in the shape of the object. The shadow is formed because you are stopping some of the rays of light from reaching the wall. Shadows are also formed in sunlight. This is a shadow.

Zoetrope

A zoetrope is a cylinder with a series of pictures round the inside which seem to move when you spin it.